DHARMA RASA

DHARMA RASA

Kuldip Gill

NIGHTWOOD EDITIONS

Published by
NIGHTWOOD EDITIONS
RR #22, 3692 Beach Avenue
Roberts Creek, BC Canada
V0N 2W2

Cover design and illustration by Kim LaFave
Author photograph by Jim McIntosh
Printed and bound in Canada

Nightwood Editions acknowledges the financial support of the Government of Canada through the Canada Council for the Arts for its publishing activities.

Canadian Cataloguing in Publication Data

Gill, Kuldip, 1934–
Dharma rasas

Poems.
ISBN 0-88971-170-4

I. Title.
PS8563.I47976D52 1999 C811'.54 C99-910962-6
PR9199.3.G52985D52 1999

For my family

and in memory of my parents,

Bhagwant Kour Gill (1914–1980)
Indar Singh Gill (1901–1969)

CONTENTS

PART I

SRINGARA RASA
Eros

LOVE LETTERS—CANADA TO INDIA, 1930s

Can I live this love, matching you to poetry
in Urdu, Gurmukhi and Hindi,
and have as reply only your few unlettered
lines telling me that our children are well,
relating my mother's love and brother's wife's whine?

I wait. No letters. Not even paper-love rewards.
Chained to pulling green lumber all night, dragged
through black sleepless nights, thoughts of
your long green eyes, your face, blaze my mind.
My children's voices cry/laugh through my dreams.
Enfeebled by endless greenchain shifts, I fear
a war, the years.

No passports yet? Fathom my heart's great dukh. I watch.
Droves of birds fly away together, another winter.
Come before the war, come through Hong Kong and Yokohama.
Please let me know as soon as you can.
And I will send money to Moga
to bring you, the children, across
the kala pani to Victoria.

Come soon. Before the war.
I'll tell you what you will need to bring:
sweaters for the children, books,
seeds, are hard to get. Bring yourself. Yourself,
and surma for your beautiful green eyes.

I am your beloved Inderpal Singh,
who would spread flower petals for you,
and fly to you on feathers, if I could.

OUD JA KALYA KAUVA (FLY AWAY BLACK CROW)

She sings the old songs, pulling her shawl
closely to cover her head as she winnows the grain,
tossing the chaff aloft to the skies. The simple lines,
filmi geet from Hindi movies echoing
her wistfulness and love, she sings,

Oud ja kalya kauva
theno kao-the-chewree pauhma.

Fly away black crow, and I
will feed you rotis crushed
in melted butter.

Remembering the husband-emigrant
the Kala (black) Kama (god of love)
gone too long, and she, enmeshed
in thick webs of a clan's familial life,
in bondage to a mother-in-law,
in purdah from lecherous red-eyed men,
is her own children's slave.

Envious of the women who carry
food to husbands in the field,
she watches the tassels of corn whirl
where couples are seduced by shade.

MY EYES HURT WHEN YOU'RE NOT HERE

(A husband in Canada to his nineteen-year-old wife in India)

I walk alone from the mill, covered with hemlock,
cedar sawdust, pitch, slivers in my skin.

Are these the stars I saw reflected in your eyes every night
as you lay beside me on the charpi outside?

Do your sahelis tease your sorrowful eyes as they sing
ghazals, bolian, love songs at weddings?

Do the flowers of the chameli spread like a carpet in the
bagh remembering we walked whispering dusky words?

This jindgi I offer to you, the sawdust, cedar and hemlock—
hair shirt my anger/longing for you subsides.

Your absence walks in the memories I left,
preceding my steps.

A ghostly figure in the fog.

THE DREAM TRAIN

You walk toward me, greet me, take me
to the food-seller's hut. We eat fresh yogurt
in cool clay bowls, sweet and mud-dusky.

You say, Come with me, rest before the next train.
It's safe, I'm Brahmin, an engineer,
a yogi.
Come rest?

I go with you,
bathe in shadow-cooled well water.
Rest in this cool room
on the first floor, farthest from the sun.

Long black hair glistening, water drawn from the well,
you shine wet. Unmixed drops of oil and water slide down
your burnished body. Cool sacred threads, dark,
damp, hang across your twice-born chest.
I watch,
rest.

I watch you meditate, show your calm look
like that white broody peace dove
hovering, wings flapping over you.

You sit cross-legged on the floor
chant a roll call,
euphonic litany of Vedic gods: Aum Aum A . . . u . . . m . . . . .

You look into my eyes, eyes wide, subtle
state of bliss, and desire, entranced
yogic posture,
straight-backed body.
You arch towards me, desire subdued by
boundless yogic power,

shake your head side to side, send your words
across the room to the bed where I rest, wait
for you to catch your breath,

words never heard before.

Ancient ways melded to sacred yogic gaze
looking up from the floor,
            prophetic:

                    You . . . are Shakti!

I am woman,
no woman was ever more Shakti
than that moment. I knew I had no need
of food. Surprised, you offered burlapped ice,
cooled mangoes, small red bananas to eat.

You call the rickshaw-wala,
ask, Shall I take you to the train?

Come with me. Take me
to the train.
You give my bags to the porter, say goodbye,
just that
and walk away,
your full-muscled body gleaming,
hair curled around your head.
My stomach knotted.
Put me on the train.

You . . . are Shakti

runs through my head,
sensual, erotic, full as woman,
mulled every day since.
My body sings the memory of heat,
the cool room, your water-and-oil wet body,
clinging black hair.
I rest, climb aboard
the dream train again.
Again. Voluptuous, delicious, tantric, licentious. Again
Shakti-full thought trains.

LOVE SONG

Bring the bulbul's song,
his eyes black like silk.
Let his heart throb under my ear.

As coverlet for my breasts
let him unknot his ebon hair.

Then my sighs of cardamom, cloves
and honeyed cinnamon
will wisp under his tongue,
lick his mouth and full-lipped sounds.

KILDEER'S DANCE

Gold-fantailed, black-pleated Kathakali dancer,
your feathered feet thrum the ground,
wings make mudras,
symbolic gestures, and
circle, circle the grassy mound.

A sweeping turn, one lowered wing glides,
sweeps tufts, flicks pebbles
while your feet alternate drumming sounds
faster and faster, singing: sweet, tsweet, tsee.
Circle, circle the Kildeer hen.

Thrumming calls, mates flutter,
hearts, heads lowered, shy.
Shakti, Kildeer replies, watches
both contenders enter, dash
swoop, feet drum: phat, phat, phat.

Kathakali dress-like feathers, his fantail pleats,
sudden gusts, subtle cool breezes,
feet stamp: kathak, kathak, kathakali.
The ménage à trois
lifts, flies swift
in an urgent triangle
towards the sun, crisp feathers,
a phoenix.

Only two return, circle and circle,
their ice blue eggs nested in a grassy mound,
dance potent circles: kathak, kathak, kathakali.
The sun-edged feathers,
red hot ring, blaze on.

KARUNA RASA
Sorrow

SAMARAN

I. Hand to Hand to Hand: Would Theirs Be a Life to Disregard?

I hold your letters in two hands,
as when in the temple receiving prasad.
Letters written by my father to my mother,
a man in Canada to his young wife in India.

His hands wrote these lines,
her hands held these letters,
her eyes eked meanings from the sounds
of his words, from between the lines.
Letters read first by his mother,
sister, brother, someone who could
read them fast, get the message, get the tone.

She read them last, slowly,
eking out each sound,
e-a-c-h v-o-w-e-l
To hear his voice,
to remember how he strung his words,
breaths and sighs, long sounds
and breaks. She melted words, riddled
meanings, for her, alone.

She read them like this
on rose-pink sleepless mornings
before the house woke,
at the peacock's first shriekings;
she read them in moonlight haze,
on starlit nights, as sheet lightning
filled the skies.

She folded and unfolded,
reading the words of a lovesick Canadian husband.
Eventually, she tied them into packets,
placed them locked in boxes
in her trunk. Brought them back to him
with children's sweaters, seeds and chooran and saffron,
the books he ordered, the surma for her green eyes,

their phulkari and their bagh.

She read them even in the madness,
when days and nights ran into screams and fits
and tearless fears, the rage.
Between the tearing hair,
the self-afflicted forehead bruises,
the despair, the remorse.
In between she unwrapped and read them,
tied up and saved.

Until the sirens took her away from
him. Shouting curses in the air,
she cried, Don't let anyone near my trunk!
Keep my keys safe!

My mother's hands were younger then
than mine today. I hold the letters,
one the writer and one the reader,
the lover and the loved.
I have moved them then stored them a dozen times.
Now, I hold them in my hands.
I open them.

I have read them, Mama,
and I have discovered love.
It sustained you through those years
of madness, anger, sickness and tears, rage, lobotomy,
terror, fear, Crease Clinic, children, aloneness, despair.
It is all here:
your coal-black hair, green eyes, sweet smile.
My father loved this woman,
My mother. You.

I know because he told you so
at the start of every letter
and at the end of each, in prose,
in poetry, between the lines,
his "cluster of grapes,
pomegranate blossom,
date fruits and my Bhagwant, Bhagwant!"

In Gurmuki and Urdu, the language of the poet,
these words, his. Music.

Do letters sustain you,
do they still a heart,
hug a body,
wrap themselves around you?
Ink fades,
what happens to their between-the-lines?
These imaginings,
my insights, their outreachings?

When I die, will my death erase
my discovery,
their love?

II. Death's Messenger

He died at her feet. She, mad, as always,
screamed into the street.
The men in the truck shop
walked over—after all this was
a different cry: Come! Come, he's fallen!

He lay still. Old, just home from work, from the mill,
the cedar, hemlock, sawdust slivers hair shirt.

He said only, Oe! Rabba! and no more . . .
She couldn't see it was his dhil. He couldn't be revived.
Parted again. Kismet. She wept, alone again
and on . . . for years before she too died.

III. After Death—Love Letters

Though they sink through the sea they shall rise again;
though lovers be lost love shall not;
And death shall have no dominion.
—Dylan Thomas, "And Death Shall Have No Dominion"

Come soon, I am alone again. I'll wait for you again, bring your
surma and your green eyes, your everyday sounds, your walk and
your breath. I wait, my love, I wait. I am your prem pujari.
Afloat amongst the petals, I go again before you.
I must . . . again . . . alone . . . before you. Without you.
Oe! Rabba! I shall wait
without even words
until you arrive.

IDENTITIES: HEART AND SOUL

If I should die before I wake
retrace, applaud
my colour: wheat, a unity, at one
with a persistent personality, identity.

Say over me,
Identities are stable, fixed, whole and of a piece.
She declared hers

to people who hid their own statuses
as immigrants, denied ethnicities, whole or part,
old or new, recent or historical, as classless or full
and likewise denied engendered lives were fuller,
took strong positions but forgot
they too were in process, took part
in staged humiliations: in misspelt,
mispronounced or hyphenated names,
hated culture's colours, and noted so many
multi-axed differences that they killed
outright and forthright the epiphanies
of migration's expression of human spirit.

If I should die before I wake
say over me,
She lived within and outside, never complete,
a work progressing: samsara, karma, moksha.
A quieted heart, humiliation-iced tongue,
she wondered, in awe of senseless racist driven rages.

If I should die before I wake
say over me,
She lived, moved, knew, said more and more,
thawed a voice, spoke to a world,
damned humiliations that made some humans tap dance,
heard hollow caustic post-worlds
and eternal drums,
sought poetic music and social peace,
but she wrote, she knew and she sang the epiphanies
of the migrant's expression of human spirit.

ADBHUTA RASA
Wonder

SONJA BETI

Mama saw me, called my Aunt,
to see the baby I was carrying.
A 'glass' made of tin and nickel alloy
carried around, wrapped
in a piece of rag, I was three.

In the shade we three sat
side by side, on our charpi
there was a smell of cool damp cloth,
water-cooled dust, and shards of gold straw.

Her hands pulled the needle
and left a row of
minute white stitches behind.
A body, no bigger
around than my hand,
small arms, round
as my Aunt's little finger,
legs the size of her thumb,
she stitched almond eyes
that looked kohl-lined,
and fine etched lips.

Alive, her skin
wheat-coloured
khaki cotton.

I wrapped and carried her
around in our compound
all day, singing:

Sonja beti, haaAh auun,

haaAh auun

Sonja, mere sona, haaAh auun,

haaAh auun.

TRAVELLING THROUGH THE BORDERLANDS

Immigration officials wouldn't let us go
aboard the CPR Empress Line.
Quarantined, a whole
long month in Hong Kong.

With sty-burned eyes I held
my mother's hand tightly,
looked and
listened, as sound burned.

We stayed in the Hong Kong Sikh temple.
In the morning, a policeman standing on a pedestal whistled
at rickshaws, cars, cycles, people.

I watched two men, twins, joined at the chest
roll along the ground, each pushing
over the other with the momentum of thin arms.
Between them a coin box rattled up and down.

My mother led me up steps
flanked by carved granite lions.
Inside a glass box I saw a coiled
snake's shed skin.

I wore new shining red clogs
with nailed-on black patent leather tops
that clipped and clopped along cement sidewalks,
elevated in the rain.

Everywhere things hung on lines with strings:
pork, grizzled chickens, heaped gizzards, glazed everythings,
fish, pineapples, small red bananas, peeled tangerines,
all smelling of each other.

I wonder my mother survived without English,
illiterate twenty-three, carrying an infant boy,
a four-and-a-half-year-old girl
across oceans, month-long quarantines, continents,
head taxes, third class holds, immigration rules.

She bought a granite grinding-pestle to make masala,
two saris, a cut-velvet jacket and dress, and for her neck,
a hammered gold gingeeri to take to Vancouver.

TRANS-PACIFIC SHIPS: *The Empress of Japan*

I sing of the mother ship, *Empress of Japan,*
in whose deep womb generations swam,
in the belly, in the hold. I sing who came
before, who succored the new,
the mother and infants
travelling airless, a third-class hold.

Sojourning men knew how to light
the bunsen-burner plate and
to ignore the *Empress's* rules as before,
as she reeled up wave and down channel.

They cooked plain curry,
though stewed meat
lay hidden in mustard greens' folds
unbeknowst to innocents,
polluted for life. Though she cursed him, still
fed her son and daughter, crying.
Forever more she told how
it felt to be full; starved for Indian
food for weeks, and then to find one
who knew cookery, a badmash who added meat
on the *Empress of Japan.*

I sing of the *Empress*;
she seated us to damask gowned tables,
served crusted buns,
never-before-tasted sweet/light butter,
unlike ghi from buffalo.

Strawberry jello! Its magic enticed,
invited, a five-year-old from an Indian village.

Ruby-red shimmering jewel-block,
a white plate, a snowy damask cloth.
Her hand held a silver spoon,
entered the ruby jewel,
pushed a path through the
soft shiny nebulous mass to be

enclosed in her mouth. Wondrous sweet
clean, slithered around the tongue, emerged
between pearly baby teeth, a melting jewel
filled her mouth, slid down
the throat, etched on the tabula rasa,
the colour: jewel-ruby-red,
flavour: strawberry.

A first, jiggling
down a girl's belly,
in the third-class hold
of the *Empress of Japan.*

HAVE YOU SEEN THE RAIN IN KERALA?

In the house at night we sat on three-legged stools
under the rain-drummed roof, telling stories by lantern
light, a kerosene smell, air hot and steamy.
Grandfather, short grey-haired, walrus-moustached,
barechested, in white muslin dhoti, bare footed,
sits nobly nearby. The sisters usually tell stories, myths, tales
to take fear away; children fall sleep as they listen
midst the family sitting peacefully.
They smile reassuringly, Now sleep!
They said, You'll be surprised at daybreak.

I lie awake, tense and hot. Listen to
the unending rain. I step outside to look at the night, a
sheer curtain of rain as it falls solid, a woven tapestry of banana
leaves, black pepper vines, cashew trees, looming
coconut palms slash their wind-whipped black fronds,
occasional lightning jabs, thunderous replies.
The eye of the wind, shooting cannons of bougainvillea blossoms.
Drops as large as silver rupees splat on the mud walk
creating fast flowing rivulets freeing children's boats.

Kerala rains bring revelry, adoration, flower-decked swings,
lovers, thoughts of concubines, kings, monsoon-viewing pavilions.
Women with upstretched arms receive rain, lick drops; their
sheer saris stuck to bodies, reveal breasts, nipples,
buttocks, round, fecund and ripe as paddy fields.

Day breaks hot and steamy, banana leaves
shine in heavy sunshine streaks, the smells of red
wet earth luscious, sticky-soft and musty-full
again with green grass and hibiscus, pavizhamalli and
the erotic blue conch-shaped sankupushpam flowers.
Workers' thatched cottages, idyllic scenes: a boater rows along
a waterway hung with lush green nagalinga trees.

Rain drums, pounds—no—hammers on the roof
all through the night. Torrents so hard
and strong evoke puerilely anxious remarks.

We are glad to be inside. This timorous shaking house
has withstood decades of battering storms.
The monsoon is in full swing; this is the brief interlude.
Life goes on between howling storms, floods,
flashed sunlight days, peopled rice fields, wading women
bent double to set paddy seedlings. And birds sing
their early-day songs, as if we dreamed the
night's monsoonal urge.

A wedding party greets us at just-dawn, happy
singing women, damp and moist, hair curling out
from freshly combed-straight braids hung with jasmine
flowers, glowing saris tied high, with dampened hems,
bare mud-caked feet, gold earrings and bracelets, laugh
as they pass by, celebrating a monsoon-blessed marriage.

They ask me,

> Have you ever been in Kerala before when it rains?
> Listen, it's the time of surging, earth and sky love-making.

Kalidasa says,

> The sky on every side is shrouded by rain-clouds
> Which wear the beauty of deep blue lotus petals
> And here look like heaps of made-up-eye-salve, and
> There possess the charm of breasts of women with child.

RAUDRA RASA
Fury

ATTAR OF ROSES AND ALMONDS—QUEENSBOROUGH, 1940

In Kashmir's gardens the rose beds glow
with aromas of Shah Jehan's creamiest reds;
sellers hawk the attar of roses, and the scullers
on Dal Lake enjoy the luminous lotus,
while in town they market all the scented oils,
almond, rose and marigold

for lover's fancy, mothers' bloom-
stretched stomachs, sun-crisped hair,
friends massage each other's aching heads
and knotted muscles, baby massage, eros
and aesthete, prolonged endless romance,
and kama sutra love.

In Queensborough, a lone Sikh boy
runs crying down the middle of the street.

In grade one, I draw cats
with big circles for heads
and small ones for the rest.

I watch him run.

In grade two the teacher says to him, Go home!
Tell your mother to wash your greasy head!

Ah! But had she learned Persian
sung ghazals, read Rashid,
Sufism's songs of attar of roses,
of gulab flowers,
chameli-lit bagh,
marigolds,
scented oils
and myrrh and incense and magic
at Queen Elizabeth School
in 1940?

MY MOTHER'S LADNER FARMHOUSE KITCHEN

My urbane aunt, of a military family
(Burma-based in her youth),
here for a Christmas visit.

A kind of rush and bustle,
warm, spicy, pestled garam masala.
Mustard seed, ginger, cumin.
Washed, not a single grain lost,
of sweet saffron-steamed rice.
While Mama slipped hot almond
skins between her fingers,
then added cloves, light raisins.

My urbane aunt
walked into the pantry, saw the mouse
trapped by cheese, spun round
with a piece of Mama's
gold and blue china; it hit
the oven shelf door and cracked.

Mama looked,
rubbed her finger over
the only plate with a cracked edge,
said nothing.
Every Christmas, a regret.

INDIAN MINIATURES: ZENANA LADY AND FALCON-GENTLE

Because you shriek down,
diving at the Muslim ruler's zenana wali's
shrill call, freezing an image.
Because you grasped the gloved hand,
talons fast, taught to soar and strike
bony beaks, tweeting chirps of tits,
And you a falcon-gentle.

Falcon, who taught you to course and spy,
land on the raja's ladies' wrists as if
in play and jest, but all the while
spurs striking eyes,
your hatchet beak
shreds feathers, dove's down,
lances a rabbit's nape.

Because you heard
a mouse's squeak, couldn't resist the call,
the trap of a falconer's lady's thrill.
Because of that woman-falcon-
gentle peregrine, you sit on wrists.
Felled. While a gloved hand
shades your head, ties a hood,
feeds you at will.

BIBHATSA RASA
The gruesome

VILLAGE GIRLS IN RAJASTHAN

A first child. *A girl?*
A blanket full of shame.
A mother's hidden face.

A midwife's neglected
charge carried away by wolves
they said.

A mother-in-law's tearful
excuse: the umbilical cord
around her throat.

A nurse moans, *A girl's*
come out. The bhang-smeared
aureole suckled, an innocent mouth.

A sister-in-law's drone, *A girl* *again.*
A midwife's fingers roll
a small pill.
Bhang, slipped into an infant yawn.

A girl! A hole dug in
warm earth, filled with
milk. An old woman adds
a live girl.

A waiting
sister cries. Women's
lessons learned.

A father
clicks prayer beads, piously
pleads, God, please,
a son!

THE KASHMIRI CARPET WEAVER'S SON

You sit at the loom
beside your sibling,
pinky finger wearing the blade
that cuts the carpet strings.

Not yet five
it has begun already
this toil
this ten-hour day.
You follow the lead of those before you
your father's father's father.

The man counts
red not blue
blue not yellow
yellow not green
green not orange
orange not emerald
emerald not carmine
carmine not azure.

You hear your father's code, a subtext:
pick up string, knot, cut
string, knot, cut
string, knot.

Your baby finger already red
the callous growing as you pick up
knot
slash
a thousand strings a day.

This is your play,
Kashmiri carpet weaver's son,
to pick
and pick
these colours, codes,
these unmusical strings.

BENARES: TWO-WHEELED CARTS

The Man
Flat-decked two-wheeled cart
loaded with twenty, twenty-foot
shining pewter-coloured steel pipes,
pushed by a man's sweat-and-sun
shiny black bulging back,
legs and arms knotted, heels dug in,
neck tendons strained ridges.
Teeth bared, nostrils flared, lips taut across,
below eyebrows lifted high
by bulging eyes
stung by sweat,
buzzed by flies.

The Horse
Pointed ears, proud Arabian gait,
pulling a rickshaw, two high
wooden wheels. Held together
by a crop-carrying
turbaned rider. Leather lines,
a steel-bitted halter
between frothing teeth,
bulging eyes
stung by sweat,
buzzed by flies.

Cart and rickshaw
carry the sign,
Horn please.

THE STONE-CARRIER WOMAN—NEW DELHI

You load a reed basket filled with rocks,
you lift it on your head,
five o'clock, barely morning,
march toward the blasting heat of day.
Green cotton sari, you throw the pala
over your shoulder, tuck the end
out of the way, into the waist.

The infant just born, held by her
four-year-old sister (already much older),
waits on-site, in the pit, on a string cot,
waits in the heat. You stop at ten,
wipe a dust-grey sweat-streaked face
with the sari's end, take the infant,
bare a dripping breast to the dry mouth.

The child sits beside you, stroked by sun,
silent, leaning on your warmth, content,
without food or water. This brief respite,
no women's decadal promises, amnesties,
or human rights.

A laser-hot sun's the sign,
you climb down into the pit,
load a reed basket head-high, lunge
in your sharp-elbowed granite.
The cement-mixer spews a grey
building's bare bones all day.

Noon sun blazes on, the child
rolls the crying infant on the ropes
of the charpi bed in the pit's heat. You stop.

First the breast for the infant's yowling,
then unroll your roti, break it,
feed the four-year-old bite by bite.
Lie down to rest, infant next to you,
lying against the child.
A green sari-shrouded family, on a charpi

in an ovenly pit, a soon-to-be-advertised
five-star international hotel.

Will the ghost of your plight
waken the tourist, the business man, as he sleeps
in lush rooms of the international
hotel whose base your bones shore?

MURMURS OF MURDER: SHE CROSSED THE KALA PANI

My male and female relatives
sat in separate rooms.
We children caught
whispered murmurs
as we went from room to room,
in our liminal state, learning.

Men:
He brought her from India,
paid her way.
He was grizzled, hoary.

Yes.
She had skin like the moon,
an exquisite ruh, and was seemly.

Wrongs? No, we don't know of others.
Nothing else.
But this thing she did.

She saw another man, a gubhru, yes.
It's a thing of izzat.
She took that away, his izzat.

He drowned her one night,
in the Fraser it's said.

We girls gulped, clutched each other
wide-eyed and afraid.

Yes, he had the right.
She was the culprit,
the wrongdoer, immoral.

God, our little brothers even nodded,
they're so silly.

Women:
She was so young, a narm village girl,
na parhe/likhe, matiar si.

He brought her here, bought her they said,
a poor family's hopes, a mother's dread.

Alone, no other women,
a shack on the millsite.
Alone, nowhere to go, voiceless.
How did she learn to live here, young, a matiar?
An ancient mill, an old man, a shack, alone.
She was exquisite. In the newspaper, black and white.

My uncle is so bad, he cut out her picture
and put it in his wallet. Don't tell my dad.

The shame. Her name and his izzat gone.

She must have stolen something, we whispered.
What is izzat? Why is Mom feeling sorry about that?

And, wasn't he young, and a gubhru they say.
Don't even say so, someone might hear you.

When I hear gubhru,
I can't even think
of handsome can you?
We tittered at our language.

He was too old to marry her, to bring her here,
to make her cross the unholy, feared kala pani.

Twice! She crossed black waters
twice, for him.

Once safely;
last, violently.

Goosebumps on our arms, the thought of
the blood, her throat, his hands, the bubbles
in the river, and the sand—when they find her
she would be covered in sand.

Would we ever do what she did?

I would never steal anything!

YOUR FIRST MOTHER

Mama,
you always called her formally, your first mother.
Let me believe she was of the family, honoured.
My sister's (really half sister's) mother.

You never told us anything about the one who was first,
how she died. (I always thought I was adopted.) I wasn't.
My father's unblinking eyes never met ours
on lives lived, not disclosed.

You taught me silence, taught me not to ask. Her name unknown,
dead, neither sadness, sounds or tears arose to mark it.
You taught me silence, taught me death.

You were a poor second wife. Your lot,
a widowed Canadian (British subject) Jat caste
husband, a grieving daughter, a careful mother-in-law.

You taught me to respect my father's relatives, the men,
izzat blazoned on each one, the honoured lineage and clan.
A grandmother and five aunts.

Taia Ji,
you were old to me even when you were young,
clean shaved, and now, an ancient archive,
Khalistan-inspired turban, widespread grey beard,
fragile body, bony bird hands.

You were all young then, and he agreed to take a second wife.
You told me he smiled when you said you saw her in India,
that our 'second' mother (to whom we weren't yet born) was nice.
You couldn't say more and still show respect.

And he didn't ask. But in notes he wrote
about my sakke mother, her face, like the chand,
long green eyes, black lashes, round eyelids, like a doe.

You are eighty now, all others gone. If I don't ask
now it will be gone. How did she die?

You thought it was illness? you said, then whispered,

> . . . truths a woman should tell you! But who?
> You have a right to know. It was *his* karab kam.
> She had no one, your father, grandfather, sara tabar, pardesi si.

You told me they couldn't save her. You said,

> She bled away, hidden
> in the house. She died that way.
> Now my daughter, you know.

A man's anguish? Her love for him?
Did he know? And when? And then?
Sparse, terse, archival notes, no relief.
The questions have just begun.

A LOBOTOMY

I remember the brick Field's general store in Mission, built 1901.
The butcher twine rolls hung from the ceiling,
the oiled paper pulled out, tore along the sharp edge,
wrapped the meat in 1941.

Daughter:
You saved string. Unlocked from the edges of flour sacks,
straightened the zigzags into neat little rolls.
Folded brown papers
as only immigrant women do.

You bleached, and boiled the Ogilvies' atta imprints out,
transformed them into tea towels, sewed them into
quilt covers, stuffed them with cotton batten.

In the hospital they raised your bed,
your head up high, sparkled knots lit with light,
the knots of butcher twine.

I saw the zigzag scar shine through the bristle,
where once the coal-black hair had glistened.
Your face, ashen grey.

You reached up, your hands
fingered the knots looped
through your skull,
the knots of butcher twine.
What did they do?

Mother:
My daughter has come, where's my shawl?
It's only a towel. I wear it and I feel the knots,
the burr, the stubble. I cover my head.
I'm afraid and cold.
My parhe/likhe daughter, your eyes hollow, face a mask.
You know I'm away, relentlessly gone.
He's here, your father, he brought you to visit. He left me here,
he knew. They cut my head and sewed it up with butcher twine.
My mind now full of frozen winds.

My daughter, sit by my side, hold my hand.
They cut my head, operation hoea
I think they put something inside? My hair!
Look after your brothers; are they fine?

Your father's turban of cheera, unstarched. How sad
he looks. Let me hold your hand on my heart,
flooded full to bursting. Tears locked from my eyes.
Shanti, Vah Guru!

I'm afraid. The terror, screams, inside.
What did they do?

You must go now?
Teke ha, quoi na, thuse jao.
It's late.

VIRA RASA
The heroic

HOMELANDS—INDIA, 1972

Memory of a five-year-old, long a pardesi:
The train Delhi to Ludhiana to Moga
to Moga to Moga steam elbowed pistons,
to the homeland, the pipal tree, the swing,
the dried fire-twigs piled to a man's height,
brown birds dust-bathing, raised puffballs, dogs baying
alarmed by gypsies camping along the Grand Trunk,
the women's warnings: take care, stay inside,
they will whisk you away.

The letter said, take the rickshaw to the taxi stand,
tell him your name, name our village
and who you are the daughter of. He will know you.
And he did, called me sister, kinswoman,
and drove me to the village of my lineage, my dadke.

People stared, the children came running, dogs barked,
a servant squatted, a straw clutched in his teeth.
A woman called out, A car, a woman from outside, alone!

They said,
See how she strides, looks you in the eye,
laughs full laughs, her accented talk.
Yet, and yet, a daughter of this village.

Remember them, the men? All gone. To Canada.
Alone, their women folk still farm these lands or
lease out the best. Cull the cattle,
sell the old, milk the rest; the children
water, walk and watch them. Remember the men?
They languished here in white pajamas.
Now, crows nest in their courtyards,
their women sleep behind locked doors.

Remember? She was five when
we put her on the train! She's come back!
We called her goody then.
How we loved her!

She said,
I remember the swing in the sacred pipal tree,
the twigs torn off for toothbrushes,
the well, small birds flittering dust, raindrops so large
imploding into puddles, sending back
splashes shaped like crowns.
My mother held the door jamb
to swing over and miss the pond.
The dogs howled in the dark. I heard
the roving gypsies' songs,
felt the villagers' fears,
their pounding hearts.
They locked the doors.
What will they take?
Will we still be here at dawn?

I remember the rooftop's star-lit nights
my father carried me up by ladder;
we followed mother. There, we three slept,
whispering dreams— a future in Canada—
so uncles, aunts and siblings couldn't hear.
My mother drawing pails of water
to wash my father's kes, our bath together.
Waddi-bebbe churning butter,
crying out, Give some lassi to the poor naukar!
I remember. An imaginary homeland.

No more, young parents on the roof
watching stars at night, finally alone.
No uncles, no married aunts who came and went as
visiting village daughters. My dog long gone.
The swing taken down when they chopped
the long branches of the pipal.

What remains? The shadow
of the compound as it was, the kitchen room,
the chula, the locked pantry, the baithak
where the men sat to stay cool, to enjoy village talk.
The painted mural which Baba Vir Singh
had commissioned above the cattle stall.
My mother's sadook with inlaid mirrors

and brass, stands as it did at her marriage.
It's empty of my little-girl dresses,
proudly worn now by young nieces.

The slow turn of the wagon wheel, an ox's
slow step, an eternity. As we women ride,
the talk unpeels in slow time, skimming
in tune to the sounds of hoofed plodding feet.
Hinges creak, the morning sounds
as farmers unlatch doors, load wagons for the day
to coax their sun-cemented fields. A granthi reads
the Guru Granth Sahib over the village microphone
at four a.m., waking the peacocks that strut
along the compound walls screeching and preening
as they peck the wheat scattered the night before.

The old men come to visit. Tell me how it was then.
The women nostalgic about how it is to live
in the lineage, the men long gone—
say, With what difficulty we have
carried out each long dhin.
I'm not like them. They say I walk like the men.
Why don't you wear jewelry? All women must
each day declare a husband's alive. And
didn't you have to marry? Don't you care?
Well, perhaps, after all it may be that you
are saved from all this. And softly,
Sister, you are lucky to have it so.

I saw it. The memories dreamlike, opaque,
strange. I came, willing to act
like a Punjabi-Sikh village daughter.
As well as I could. But what must I do
to belong in this place, here and now? Perhaps,
grow out my hair, wear a salwar/kamiz,
laugh less loud, change my walk. Dress and adornment
count—learn the ways—stay at home,
cook, become a malan and all of that?

And what about that Kanada side? We came.
Crossed the kala pani, the men

brought their singhainis.
If they raise their children there,
who will inherit the India jameen?
Is Kanada a homeland, the children's des?

Will the sight of a brown sparrow dust-bathing
in Sacramento fill a heart that yearns,
that longs for her Punjabi scenes?

Exile. On the banks of the panch ab
does the vina play no more? No!
Oh! Nathu Wala! I echo Psalm137.

> If I forget you, O Jerusalem,
> let my right hand forget her cunning . . .
>
> let my tongue cleave to the roof of my mouth,
> if I do not praise Jerusalem.

For as long as Saraswati's hand plucks the vina,
my mouth enhalos Nathu Wala,
the Punjabi plains.

THE INDIA CHEST

Mama always sat us down before her
when she opened the India chest,
showed us embroidered bagh,
phulkari cloths, chadars, saris,
family letters and masala spices,
talked a bit about everything.
We sat in awe of what she said,
of what she showed us:
the beauty of jali embroidery
colours she dyed, indigo, amber, gulabi,
and the alchemy
of hundreds of bits of mirrors covering cloth,
reflecting us.

She told us about our waddi-bebbe
our bhua and taia in our lineage,
of how we carried out our sekeria,
our relationships, arranged marriages
(there are four sets of kinsmen you can't marry)
and how we lease our lands. We can go anywhere
in this world, our roots are always with us.

She put them back into her peti,
taking care we learned to fold
letters, tapestries and cloths along
old lines, pressed,
locked in.

SHOES

Is *that* the only thing I have to write about
those days? Alienation, loneliness,
greenchain work: six-by-sixs and eight-
by-twelves pulled all day long? Leather
aprons and hands pierced with splinters?

They were men with many things on their
minds, in process, emergent. Immigrants
in a new place trying to fit in, they told each
other endless stories about each day.

My old uncle said,

> About my shoes—the soles were gone,
> we were poor. But one man, my uncle,
> against caste rules bought a shoe repair kit;
> he learned to mend our shoes.
> When I came back to the bunkhouse from the mill,
>
> He said, Hey there, son, give me your shoes.
> He sat and fixed the holes, added new laces,
> rubbed them with cold water and dubbin.
>
> Each shift of men watched him, humbled;
> they ate their meals, came and went.
> A devout Sikh. We listened, learned
> about izzat, dharma and kismet from him.
>
> He sewed our shoes, mended the leather
> aprons we used on the greenchain. That year
> my father died, I was sixteen,
> my beard just starting to come in.

Our pioneers were more than bunkhouse
men, cheap labour, head-taxed in.
They were fathers, brothers, uncles, cousins,
related men of lineages and clans who socialized
each other. They wrote letters, ghazals, sang
songs, laughed, played cards, worked and cried.

They had their responsibilities, and despite
the *Komagata Maru* incident, being pushed around,
called names, and kept out of jobs,
believed in izzat, their dharma, and kismet.

THE CANDY MAN

A glimmer of smile behind a beard, strands
of white and gold, like a hand spread across his chest,
tipped wool. The turban wrapped big and loose,
peasant style without the dandy's safa down the back
or the scholar's elegant tip of colour at the forehead.
Trousers tied with twine, cracked leather shoes
shining between the fissures. Sun-glazed
brown eyes, rimmed cataract blue, floating in
yellowed whites. A shrunken old Sikh man
on a farm, rare and flockless as a flicker.
How does he come to be here?

Friday. The country store cashes his cheque.

> *In India small hands reached out to him*
> *for candies, humbugs, gum and licorice sticks.*
> *He longs to see their glittering eyes,*
> *sticky lips, joined palms.*

East Delta. A one room school, a ditch,
the wire fence. Behind it older children
gleefully chant,

> *Hindu Pindu Pandy,*
> *come and give me candy.*

Over and over, as he flings it to them
he repeats in Punjabi,
mitthai kalo, mitthai kalo.

From his breast pocket he pulls a crumpled
paper with a small soot-smudged handprint
In broken English he says,
India letter, my daughter send it.
Holds it out with two hands.

A girl reaches through the fence
and softly fits her palm onto it.

HAY BEDS AND BRICK CHULAS, 1914–1915

In Memory of Naranjan Singh Gill, Canadian

His cousin,
Uncle Ganga's father, died at Hillside Mill,
had worked the greenchain beside him.

Grandpa, worked the vines, picked tomatoes,
stacked, slept on hay,

wore the same pants, turban, shirt
and shoes, day in, night out

from farm to farm, took the day's dirt
to night's hay loft.

Farm to forest, walked the logging rail tracks.
Sojourners, found and worked the brick factory:

bricks piled straight
each night made hard beds, curved, made
into instant chulas to cook fast foods each day.

Fitted back into walls, chimneys
or just plain loads,
as new, the next day.

BHAYANKA RASA
The timorous

MY MOTHER'S INDIA AND QUEENSBOROUGH KITCHENS

India
A chula, a tandoor she made herself.
Molded clay, it fired slow. In her veins, eons
of knowing how to cook this way. She was sure.

Queensborough
An iron wood stove with a door,
a shelf, an oven, and porcelain decoration.
When the Japanese
under pressure before internment
and desperate for cash,
sold everything on the boardwalk,
she bought a white enamel stove
from her Japanese neighbour.

The stove moved to the kitchen
by the Fraser River site. White enamel polished
bright as memory, black-edged with
fear of being transported like the Japanese
entering her life too,
like Ito's.

The stove in the kitchen cooked
Indian rice, coloured saffron
for my brother's birthdays.
Japanese interned
forgotten. *Aliens.*

Until in walked Helen, red-haired,
caring, taught mama everything
about living here. Mama learned
from her to bake two-egg white cake,
in wax-paper-lined tins,
with peel grated from Ito's
Japanese oranges, in
butter icing.

THE OLD ABBOTSFORD TEMPLE:
A CHILD'S QUERIES ABOUT THE PICTURES

A two-storey temple,
stairs rising from the street sidewalk
where we stand for the Khalsa photographs,
four doors—we are casteless,
we enter from the north, south, east and west.
Out of carpeted floors a raised dais
overlaid with sumptuous cloths,
tapestries of gold, silver, embroideries: jalis
to enfold the holy book, the Guru (Granth Sahib).

Pictures line the walls,
haunt children and frighten me.
Did our Gurus walk like this?
Headless, spouting blood from an open neck,
he holds the kirpan in one hand and
his own head in the other. He walks.

Do our temples shine like that? The golden domes.
Is it real gold? Where did it come from? Who climbed up
there and was it pounded on? Laid on? Poured on?
And what about that pond? Who swims there?
Where are the swans?

Who lit the aura around Guru Nanak's head?
Will I see that kind of man, white beard, clear-eyed,
holding a falcon, in India? In our village?
In the world? But why then, not here?

Who is that man lying on the railroad track,
the *Komagata Maru* man (martyred?)
wrapped in a white winding sheet (asleep?).
The thread of his life, like railroad ties
across a country, runs yet through us all
like a dream in the blood.

THE OLD ABBOTSFORD TEMPLE: A YOUNG WOMAN REFLECTS ON THE BHOG

I hear the granthi, recite the prayer
read from the Guru Granth Sahib.
A man gracefully waves a long white-haired whisk;
impure flies must not touch the holy book.
The rhythm of his waving arm, a voice reading,
the reciting crowd, put me to sleep.

I sit on the floor in the midst of women.
We shift our weight from cheek to cheek,
lean against the walls; friends lean backs against
our knees; old ladies balance holding our shoulders
as they pass to sit with family
or friend in the throng.

Unknown children grasp at shawls,
fall into strange laps, and turn us black
and blue when they hit our heads with theirs.
We smile, suffer the little children.
As they cry for prasad, mothers shoo them
across the room to the men's side.

In the langar below, nani's, mothers,
aunts, mothers-in-law and other women
boil the chai, knead the dough, roll the rotis,
stir the rice, egg one another on: take a turn,
peel the onions, soak the tamarind, wash the
mint, dice the potatoes, squeeze the lemons.
The old aunts say,

> Don't ask the new daughters-in law,
> unmarried girls, about to be brides,
> to do this. Oh, sundar ha!

Then, let it all go to our old eyes.
And they wipe away the sting of spice,
dry their old aware eyes.
Women share stories: whispers, tears, agonies

and laughter. And the gossips are at it.
A mother agonizes,

> We fought at Independence,
> her aunts barely made it home alive, now
> she thinks it's all right to marry and even go
> to their side in Pakistan to visit!

And then music and chants from the floor
above drone through. Women call children,
wash their hands, take aprons off, cover pots
and rotis ready for lunch. It's time for the ardas,
the common prayer. Everyone goes upstairs.
Each woman covers her head, kneels at the dais,
sits on the carpet, wherever she can.

I can't understand a word the granthi chants.
The language is old Gurmukhi mixed with Urdu
poets, Hindi and maybe even Sanskrit and Pali
prose. No one explains. Perhaps few even know.
I say the prayer, Vah Guru, and
hold two hands out for prasad.

SANTA RASA
Serenity

THE CART

Six old women in purdah
sit on an ox cart.
Looking back, they roll out tales
of family, fame, love and hatred.
A seed-drill plants rows of corn,
A loom weaves a Tabriz carpet.
One seed, one stitch.

A cart wheel turns,
presses down
the seconds, minutes, hours
to bake the
muddied ruts
in clay.

SANCTUARY

Oasis of trees and rocks, a few long benches with slatted backs bleached silver as birch, a cast of grey, white and green, anchored in concrete. Shaded by pine, hemlock and tall sharp firs, while knobby spruce throw dark shadows, their green turned black, like the home of black-tent nomads. Underneath, a startling coral azalea. One new tip of bud, almost evergreen with fine hairs, glistens like her infant, freshly veined, when the just-turned woman, the *matiar* vine maple, shifts her posture to the breeze and filters the sun's shaft through sheer leaves.

The path, from the dark tent of my sanctuary, curls around the stream, continues past me and the bench, and is a fine crushed granite gravel, sparkling white and black, mottled with pine needles, edged with the odd fern trying to grow through without interruption.

One single dandelion head stands upright, angry, staring like the demon Kali, her tumult of hair all blown away.

BLUE HERON—RUSKIN, B.C.

A leggy blue heron on the plateau of a post,
a lotus base rising from the flooded field
spread with water lily pads,
perches in the first pink light of morning;
a Monet "Water Lilies" hangs in San Francisco's Golden Gate Park;
a white horse on a bank in the South Pacific
rises above a Fijian lagoon full of magenta coloured lotuses;
1000 folded Japanese cranes, atomic bombs;
the gold and green wallpaper in a bathroom.
Shiva's perpetual dance, drummed eternally.

Your immutable one-legged stance, shielded from it all,
a long blue-grey streak with a pointed beak,
unblinking eyes,
amidst morning water lilies.

HASYA RASA
The comic

ESL DIALOGUE: TWO VOICES

I asked you to keep saying
on the bus
on the way to Woodward's store
so you could tell the clerk,

> **I** want a mousetrap.
> I **want** a mousetrap.
> I want **a** mousetrap.
> I want a **mousetrap.**

Why did you say to the clerk, I want a rat peetie?

> I forgot how to say *mouse*
> but remembered how to say *rat.*
> Ranjit and I died laughing
> on the bus.

When your friend
took the bus
to see the doctor,
you told him to keep repeating
so he could tell the secretary,

> **I** want to see Dr. Drummond.
> I **want** to see Dr. Drummond.
> I want **to see** Dr. Drummond.
> I want to see **Dr. Drummond**.

Why did he say to the clerk, I want to see Dukdhad Dhaman ?

He's the only guy I know
who ever believed
you pump a cow's tail
to get milk.

DISSEMBLED

Boring Friday, midnight in Mission Town
finished Michener's *Hawaii,*
ironed the salwar/kamiz,
Flipping through *Saturday Night,*
should begin *Bridge of San Luis Rey.*
Listening to jazz, Charlie Parker, Anita O'Day.

Outside, the gate slams shut. Two pair of footsteps,
a war whoop, and the door flies open.
In walk my teenage brother
and this long drink of water,
Ozarks-type sort of crazy logger.
Both drunk, beer in hand.

Hey, Kuldip, can we get something to eat?
Oh! Slim, meet my sister.

Slim scratches his head,
draws himself up to a string-bean six-foot-six,
adjusts his plaid work shirt collar,
drunkenly squints his eye,
leans towards his "pardner"
and slowly drawls,

Hey Stan, she speak English?
Oh yeah, Slim! She speaks good English!

I am *other,*
an Indian woman, dissembled,
explained, even by my brother.

SIKH WOMEN'S DRESS CODE—QUEENSBOROUGH, 1941–1947

A dress? No, salwar/kamiz! Observe the 5 K's
Code: Kara, Kangi, Kes, a slimmer Kachi, Kirpan.
(1" embedded in the kangi will do.)
And a slip, no burnt bras, wear them tight.
Chuni-covered heads, rakabied feet
(called here, high-heeled shoes), and a coat.

Dress Code or be called
an alien,
a Hindu,
just off the boat.

SIKH MEN'S DRESS CODE—QUEENSBOROUGH, 1941–47

A turban, no way out of it! The granthi said so.
Sikh men observed it
Code: Kara, Kanga, Kes, Kacha, Kirpan.
(1" embedded in the kanga will do.)

No pajama/kurta; in India modern
men wear pants, shirts, shoes and suits.
Canadian Sikhs carry a card that says, Alien
as the Germans and Italians do.
On our street sirens screech and wail.

A Sikh air raid warden wears the 5 K's, a black armband,
scours the street. Lights out! Lights out!
Draw down rolled tar paper blinds.
Beware the Japanese bombers!
Queensborough safety demands pitch black night.

Dress Code or be known by Sikhs as
one who cut his kes:
smokes and drinks, gambles,
carries liquor into the temples,
chases women.
Forgets to send money home,
and to write to his mother.
Has anything been left out?

SCORPION

Your temerity
in the shower room,
the tourist bungalow
(in Mahabalipuram, or
was it Puri?). You lurked
unnoticed for the moment
and I, alone, undressed
and turned the water on.

Then there you were, black,
half arched, sliding
sideways along the wall.
You stopped and
I was astonished.

Calmly finished my bath
with one eye on you,
the other on the door.

I turned off the water,
wrapped myself in a lungi
and ran shivering
to the bedside phone.

I called the front desk,
Send the dhobi
there is a scorpion
on my wall!

Two days later
a boy appeared
carrying a fly swatter.
He took your carcass,
my reluctant kill.

A VERY PROPERLY KILLED CHICKEN

Catch it as it flaps and squawks,
put the head on a block, and to mesmerize it,
draw three lines in front of its eyes.

Chop hard and fast, let go, watch it
osterize the air with blood, running—
wings on the go, head apart on the block,
eyes bright, tongue still flapping.

Chop off the feet and wing tips, skin it. Open it, take out
the innards fast. Place the heart on a white plate.
Watch it beat!

Dice the gizzard,
add the heart, still throbbing,
simmer stew, potatoes, onions, cilantro.
Watch the ladies hands slip-slapping rotis.
Watch them serve the men.

The kitchened women spurn
men's appetites, properly
and brazenly
eat carrots, potatoes, onion
and eggplants, hot rotis, dripping
butter, cucumber yogurt,
mango chutneys and
kheer.

PART II

KULDIP KE DIVAN: GHAZALS

GHAZAL I

The Punjab plains, pink plumes of sugar cane stalk, the dust storm
crackles, razor grasses, whisks of white-bearded pampas.

A nairee! They come, dervishes on the wind! Pillage the poorest village.
Dreaded dacoit hidden in thickets.

White-eyed horses, bit-stretched mouths. Lightning legs, hooves, manes.
Crops across wet flanks. Knotted white knuckles.

Lock and bolt doors and gates; blow out dia. Hide, women! Hide!
Vasanti says, Nairee aiee ha! Dacoit thirst, red-eyed, for women.

GHAZAL II

My loves are dying. Or is it that my love
is dying, day by day, brief life, brief candle.
—Phyllis Webb, *Water and Light*

A pair of hawks. Undeciphered language, meaningless
as their patterns of flight. Love with no owners.

Mirages. Desires, the pink shadows of the desert. Buddha
mocks their intensity, everything is dukh.

Metal turned to stone, the alchemist's yearning. A woman's
pouting lips, the clefts in her ox's hoof. A metal twist-tie heart.

Aquarian, I turn myself into wind: sirocco, levanter, simoom,
worse than a storm at sea. Deserts, oceans, stars, the moon: me!

Stalking out of her depth, there is Vasanti
There! Riddles yet to solve.

GHAZAL III

I asked the rose at dawn, how did the bulbul in affliction fare?
It pointed to some feathers that lay scattered in the garden: There.
—from the poet Mir

Twenty-five stories, and each day the beggar's fruit.
Unostentatious, it awaits the monkey's mouth.

Men will desire, tamper, consume, destroy, unbridled.
The pericarp of the fruit, the graveyard tree's.

An amusing innocence. The click of circumstance, the gem inside.
The monkey's somersault. Now what? Now what? Abandoning.

A girl! Brilliant jewel of a seed. A special fruit.
Here is your mango: I am the beggar. Yet you uncover nothing.

Karma's playful touch, the burst of fate from the eternal store.
The negative silk of nothingness. Vasanti! Your ballet slippers.

GHAZAL IV

Brahma sleeps; we are his dream. Awakening, he ends kali yuga.
Maitreya, Mahavira and Brahma come again. Don't tread on his egg!

Zimmer, it is true. The past we damned hangs in the tree; we fetch it
again and again. The obvious is only semblance, the hidden, real.

I needs *We* to discover *I*. Dorn again, yolk of Olson, Here Kums the
Kosmos dont just stand there lookin dumb stick out your thumb!

A peacock's colours streak the pea-hen's yolk. Oh! A poet's words
are true streams, parented. Source: Brahman, and sound burns.

Love? I, Sati, lay in fifty-two sacred places, worshipped, here, here, and
there. Shiva's a lingam of stone, dance and anklet bells stilled.

GHAZAL V

My white mare on the Punjabi plains, the stamp of her hooves
marks the borders of my land as she is turned loose.

It's the morning of her wedding. How tightly they braid her hair.
Now her doria are swinging; in hours they will be his, turned loose.

A swing hangs in the pipal tree. Baisaki: flowers yellow and gulabi.
From the roof top khoti the cucurooing doves have been turned loose.

The white stallion savours a mouth without bit and bridle.
Off with his saddle! A slap on the flanks and he is turned loose.

The doli swings as guests watch the bride leave her natal village.
Bristling with coir, the coconut in the groom's lap is turned loose.

Awake Vasanti! His imposters under gowns of virtue. On love's
wings, the phoenix by his flaming heart is turned loose.

GLOSSARY

ab river.
ardas prayer.
atta wheat flour used to make roti.
aum (or om) a sacred utterance symbolizing the universe, a mantra.

badmash trickster, a con man.
bagh garden or agricultural field, a cloth embroidered with flowers.
baisaki spring festival.
baithak a place where men sit; a sitting room; men's quarters.
beti daughter.
bhang hemp.
bhog temple ceremony.
bhua aunt (father's sister).
bolian folk songs, sometimes somewhat bawdy when sung at weddings.
Brahma an Indian deity.
Brahman the impersonal, absolute, divine power.
bulbul an Indian nightingale.

chadar a sheet.
chai Indian tea made with milk and sugar.
chameli a beautiful spreading floral plant.
chand the moon.
charpi a small stool with a woven seat.
cheera a special sheer Indian cotton, often with a diagonal pattern.
chooran a medicinal powder.
chula a hearth, often describing the commensal group.
chuni a headcovering, also called a dupatta.

dacoit a petty robber, a thief, often part of a roving band.
dadke relatives on the father's side.
des the home country; the native land.
dharma a complex value-laden term containing moral virtues such as religion, righteousness, law, duty, and faith. It is also linked to the stage of one's life (ashrama).
dhil heart.
dhin day.
dhobi one of the washermen caste.
dhoti a wrap for the lower body worn by men.
dia a small lamp.

doli very sad wedding songs, also the cart that carries a bride away.
doria decorative wool or cotton extensions for braids.
dukh existential pain or sorrow.

filmi referring to Indian film.

garam hot.
geet song.
ghazal special form of poem using a Persian and later, Urdu structure.
ghi clarified butter.
gingeeri a necklace.
granthi priest.
gubhru a fine young man.
gulabi rose colour.
gurdwara Sikh temple.
guru teacher, spiritual guide.
Guru Granth Sahib sacred text of the Sikhs.

hoea has become, from the verb to be.

izzat a code of family honour, respectability, moral integrity and social standing.

ja go (s. imperative).
jali a special form of open embroidery work.
jameen land.
jao go (p. imperative).
jindgi life.

kacha underpant (m.), one of the five Sikh symbols.
kachi underpant (f.), one of the five Sikh symbols.
kala pani "Black water," or ocean. Since ancient times Indians are religiously enjoined not to cross it.
kala yuga the fourth in the four cycles of time (eras) in Hindu (Puranic) cosmology. It is the present time. This is the most degenerate of eras which shows the failings of men and gods. It is called the Dark Age, a time of wars and terrors, etc.
Kali an Indian goddess.
kalo eat (imperative).
kalya black.
kam work.

kama god of love.
kama sutra an early Indian textbook of eros ascribed to Vatsyanyana.
kamiz a shirt-like top worn by women.
kanga comb (m.), also a Sikh symbol.
kangi comb (f.), also a Sikh symbol.
kao butter.
kara a steel bracelet, one of the five Sikh symbols.
karab bad; morally indecent.
karma destiny. A moral law that states "One reaps what one sows." One's actions have related outcomes.
kathak famous "story" dances.
kathakali classical Indian dance form, a classical dance-drama.
kauva a crow.
kes hair, unshorn hair is a Sikh symbol.
khalsa Sikh community, formally "the army of the pure".
kheer a rice and milk pudding.
khoti a small room, sometimes on a rooftop.
kirpan a Sikh religious symbol in the form of a curved knife.
kismet fate.
kurta a man's collar-less shirt.

langar the Sikh dining hall.
lassi a buttermilk drink.
likhe one who can write, or one who writes.
lungi a sarong-like wrap, or garment.

malan one who looks after the farm and animals.
masala a hot spice mixture.
matiar a young woman just entering maturity.
maya illusion.
mere my.
mitthai sweets.
mitthai kalo! eat some sweets!.
moksha release for the soul from the painful cycle of rebirths (the primary and end goal of reincarnation).
mudra complex system of hand gestures used in dance and drama.

nairee duststorm.
nairee aiee ha a windstorm has come.
narm soft or gentle.
naukar household servant.

oe! oh!.
Oe! Rabba! a pained cry: Oh! God!
oud fly.

pajama traditional men's trousers.
pala the decorated edge of a sari.
panch five.
pardesi away from the homelands.
parhe/likhe literally, reader/writer. A term used to denote a literate female person.
pauhma to feed, or to throw feed to.
peetie a trap.
peti a trunk.
phulkari embroidered cloth made for a girl's wedding.
pipal a type of tree.
prasad a sanctified food used in blessings.
prem pujari priest of love.
purdah veiling practised by women; an avoidance behaviour.

quoi na never mind.

raja a king.
rakabi high heeled shoes.
rat peetie rat trap.
rickshaw-wala one who pulls a rickshaw, one who owns a rickshaw.
roti an unleavened flatbread.
ruh a look, complexion, appearance.
rupee an Indian coin.

sadook a woman's linen chest.
safa the decorative end piece of a turban.
sakke (or *sakhi*) kin; particularly a blood relationship; a person's kindred.
salwar baggy trousers.
samaran remembrance.
samsara rebirth. Traces of indelible memory imprinted on the psyche.
sara all.
sari a woman's garment.
sekeria kin relationships.
shakti female power principle.

shanti peace.
singhainis women of the singh's, the wives of singh's.
sona gold.
sonja go to sleep.
sundar beautiful.
surma soot black powdered eye makeup.

tabar family.
taia father's elder brother (an uncle).
tandoor a clay oven.
teke ha that is right.
thainu to you.
thuse you (plural form).
thuse jao you (plural) go, you should go.

vah praise.
vedic from the vedas.
vina a stringed musical instrument.

waddi-bebbe big mother, usually a term reserved for a grandmother.
wali a word signifying belonging or ownership.

yogi an ascetic person, one who practices self denial as a way to religious discipline.

zenana wali a woman who lives in the women's apartments in the raja's palace.

NOTES ON THE TEXT

1. Rasa theory, part of Indian genre theory and Sanskritic poetics, describes an elaborate typology of nine basic emotions, each of which can be identified as the reigning tone of a work. Inspired by the breadth of this type of context and its ability to order experience, I have placed the poems in this book into sections based on the nine emotions. They are sringara (eros), karuna (sorrow, pathos, the tragic), adbhuta (wonder, delusional comforts of the marvellous), raudra (rage, fury, cruelty), bibhatsa (the gruesome or loathsome), vira (the heroic), bhayanka (the timorous or fearsome), santa (serenity, peace, quietude) and hasya (the comic). I have not explored the more than thirty-one other subsidiary emotions (jubilation, dejection, agitation, debility, weariness, indolence, etc.).

Rasa is often referred to as a sentiment, or basic stereotype. In rasa theory the emotive meaning, or the cognitive content of the work and the context and type of discourse, are important. According to Indian theory, a necessary or primary condition of a literary work is its rasa or rasadhvani (evocativeness). Daumal (1979:11) states that rasa is a savour, as in a gustatory experience, "a cognition that shines with its own evidence." Rasa is a palate of certain causes and their effects, "for those who have knowledge," as in the emotion of love (the rasayate). It is also, like food, enjoyed by gourmets, who relish victuals served with the proper condiments and a range of ingredients.

In Punjabi, rasa, in its simplest form, means the distinct flavour (as in the juice of a fruit) of an emotion, or perhaps even its inherent tone.

I use "dharma" in the religious sense of the word, as the inalterable duty of a thing or being, and as the intellectual and moral motives found in human conduct. The traditional Indian meaning is that dharma indicates the essential nature or quality of a thing. In this book the name has special meaning since the immigrant experience encloses us within the circle of dharma, which is nothing if not the epitome of transformation through the eons.

2. Many of these poems were inspired by stories told by my parents and by other family members. Some were written after reading letters that my father had written to my mother in India, which she carried back to Canada.

In 1913 when my grandfather came to Canada, there were few Sikh families in B.C. He brought his youngest son (my father) and four of his nephews to Canada. In 1939 my mother, brother and I came to Canada to join my father and grandfather. Within two years of arriving in

Queensborough, my family moved to Mission, where we were the first Sikh family in the town. My mother spoke no English. She came from a culture where women of the same clan lived together in large families, all generations under one roof. Here, we were alone. A few Sikh men also lived in Mission, and one family lived on a farm near Deroche. Few Sikhs today know what it was like to live in Canada in the early years of immigration and through World War II. Some of these poems are our stories written as poetry.

3. The "I" of the text is not necessarily the author, and some "stories" have been put together from bits of conversations, dreams and other sources such as stories or reminiscences told by others.

4. The lines above Ghazal II are from Phyllis Webb's book, *Water and Light: Ghazals and Anti Ghazals*, (Coach House Press, Toronto, 1984, p. 17). Ghazals III and IV were inspired by reading Heinrick Zimmer's *The King and the Corpse: Tales of the Soul's Conquest of Evil*, edited by Joseph Campbell. In Ghazal IV, the line "Here Kums the Kosmos dont just stand there lookin dumb stick out your thumb," is a slightly changed version of one from the first page of *Gunslinger Book III, THE WINTERBOOK prologue to the great Book IIII Kornerstone*, by Edward Dorn (Frontier Press, West Newbury, Massachusetts, 1972).

5. Any errors or omissions are my own.

ACKNOWLEDGEMENTS

Some of the poems in this book appeared in an altered version in *Event: The Douglas College Review*. "Kildeer's Dance" was published in the Poet's Signature Broadsheet series by Colophon Books in an edition of fifty numbered copies, designed, illustrated and printed by Jim Rimmer at Pie Tree Press in New Westminster. My sincere thanks to the editors.

Special thanks to Marisa Alps, my perceptive and sensitive editor—I deeply appreciate her insights, support and encouragement; to Howard White and his team at Harbour/Nightwood for trust; and to David Zieroth and Robert Adams for their respect and keen editorial advice and comment on this book. Rosemary Nixon read an earlier version of this manuscript and commented on most of these poems, and I thank her.

I thank the following: the students in the UBC Creative Writing Department, especially instructors Kate Braid, Keith Maillard and George McWhirter; UBC's Booming Ground Writer's Community (1999) and Dionne Brand; The Banff Centre; Susan Musgrave at the Poemcrazy Workshop at Mothertongue Press, Salt Spring Island; Co-op Radio's "Radiofreerainforest" (1999); the Fraser Valley Regional Libraries in Abbotsford, Maple Ridge, White Rock and North Surrey, for sponsoring readings (1998); Calliope, my women's writing group, for their nurturing; and Mona Fertig, for advice and support. Many other people have been generous in this process and I thank them.

I would like to thank Jim McIntosh for love, advice and support. Thanks to my brothers, Kal, Stan and Jerry Gill and their families. Special thanks to Lorelle (our newest poet), Candace, Dana, Lindsay, Jasmine, Kira, Cassidy and Nicholas. Their story times and lullabies taught me to value cadence and rhythm.